Costantino Guerra

ALL FLORENCE

235 COLOR PHOTOGRAPHS
CITY MAP

BONECHI EDIZIONI "IL TURISMO"

INDEX

Revised edition 2003

Copyright by Bonechi Edizioni "Il Turismo" S.r.l.
Via dei Rustici, 5 - 50122 FLORENCE
Tel. +39-055.2398224/25
Fax +39-055.216366
e-mail: info@bonechionline.com
        bbonechi@dada.it
Internet: http://www.bonechionline.com
Printed in Italy
All rights reserved

Photographs: Bonechi Archives; Rolando Fusi; Piero Bonechi; Marco Rabatti
and Serge Domingie; Giuliano Valsecchi (K&B News): page 91, on top.
Cover: Paola Rufino
Reprohouse: Bluprint Srl., Florence
Print: STIAV S.r.l., Florence
ISBN 88-7204-055-8

HISTORY

The origins of Florence go back to the Etruscan epoch, when Fiesole dominated the valley from its hill. Groups of inhabitants went down to the banks of the Arno to found a village, modest, but destined to thrive, thanks to its favourable position on the direct line of communication between the north and south of Italy; although this did make it more vulnerable by enemy attack and invasion. The Romans soon founded a colony here with the auspicious name of Florentia (that is, destined to flourish). Already in the 2nd century B.C. the new municipality had acquired a position of pre-eminence among the cities of the Roman *Tuscia*. The town survived the Dark Ages to emerge slowly in the Carolingian epoch. First the feud of the Marquises of Tuscany, among whom Ugo and Matilda should be recorded, from the 11th century onwards Florence began to acquire greater and greater autonomy; in 1115, after the struggles against the simoniacal clergy and the feudal lords of the surrounding neighbourhood, the Florentine Comune had virtually come into being; ten years later the new state defeated her rival, Fiesole. Soon, inside the city, now surrounded by a new circle of walls, the first clashes began to take place between im-

migrant overlords and the artisan class, organised into the extremely powerful Guilds and Trade Corporations. These clashes created the two factions of the Guelphs (who supported the Pope) and the Ghibellines (who favoured the Emperor) with the distinct prevalence of the former. After the end of the 13th century the Guelphs themselves divided into two parties of "black" and "white", which had split up on the basis of a long-standing rivalry; the black party, supported by the Pope, sent the white partisans into exile in 1303; these included Dante Alighieri. In the meantime Florence was becoming more powerful, fighting against rival cities (Pistoia, Arezzo, Volterra, Siena) and expanding her territory. Also in the cultural and economic fields, at the turn of the 13th-14th century she was becoming, one of the most important centres in Italy. This was the period of the great companies of bankers and merchants, when the wool and silk industries were flourishing. In 1348 there was a terrible outbreak of plague, described by Boccaccio at the beginning of the *Decameron*. The last decades of the 14th century saw increasingly violent clashes between the *popolo grasso*, the rich middle class which ruled the state by means of the Guilds, and the *popolo minuto*

Panorama from the Cascine Park, by Gaspare Vanvitelli (Museo di Firenze com'era).

Recent excavations in Piazza della Signoria; facing page: *detail of the fresco by Vasari in Palazzo Vecchio, depicting Florence during the siege of 1530.*

or working class. The struggle came to a head in the *Tumulto dei Ciompi* (humble carders in the Wool Guild) by means of which the lower classes of the citizenry came to power (1378). But soon afterwards the oligarchy headed by the Albizi regained the ascendancy by supporting the small populace; the rich Medici family was acquiring increasing political importance, and soon the rule of the Signoria was established, although republican appearances were preserved. Cosimo the Elder, who founded the Medici rule, was succeeded by Lorenzo the Magnificent, a shrewd statesman and a great patron of the arts. The century that culminated in the rule of the Magnificent (died 1492) is one of the most brilliant in Florentine history, especially in the field of culture and art; it was the century of Humanism and the great art of the Renaissance. Between the end of the 15th and the early 16th century the city had a free Republican government, after the expulsion of Piero, the successor to Lorenzo. This period is dominated by the figure of Girolamo Savonarola. After the Medicis returned, Florence remained under their rule until 1527, when a fresh revolt restored the Republican institutions. But the Medicis, supported by the Emperor and the Pope, returned once more after a harsh siege (1530). Despite the political unrest, the years between the end of the 15th century and the first decades of the 16th century were rich in great personalities in the artistic and literary fields (Michelangelo, Machiavelli, Guicciardini). In 1569 Cosimo dei Medici, the ruler of the city, received the title of Grand Duke, which he passed on to his successors. After Cosimo his son Francesco I acceded to the government of the city; a lover of art and letters, he had little propensity for ruling. The following century saw the beginning of the city's decline; international factors (the preponderance in Europe of the great powers of France, Austria and Spain; the shift northwards of the centres of economic power) and the lack of significant personalities among the Medici Grand Dukes, with the exception of Ferdinando II, all combined to exclude Florence, as for that matter the whole of Italy, from the category of European powers. The extinction of the dynasty with Gian Gastone (1737) and the passing of the Grand Duchy to the Lorraine family, connected with the ruling Austrian house, allowed Florence to recover a certain marginal importance in Europe. The Lorraines ruled the Grand Duchy, except during the period of Napoleonic domination (1799-1814), until the union of Florence and Tuscany with Italy (1859). Florence was the capital of the new kingdom from 1865 to 1871. The city continued to be, as it is now, a lively artistic and cultural centre.

5

The Cathedral and Giotto's Bell Tower; facing page: *the facade of the Cathedral.*

PIAZZA DEL DUOMO

At the dawn of the Middle Ages, the site of the Piazza was a mass of dwelling houses and public buildings. The church of Santa Reparata was built over the foundations of one of these latter in the 4th century. Three centuries later (though some think in the same century) the Baptistry was erected next to the church, and this place began to form the centre of religious life in Florence. Santa Reparata became a cathedral in 1128. The church was becoming too small for this new role and greater dignity — the population was increasing too — and in 1289 the Comune decided to enlarge it. This was part of an extensive rebuilding plan that involved the widening out of the city walls (the Roman circle was too small), the construction of a Priors' Palace (now Palazzo Vecchio) and alterations to existing buildings such as Santa Croce, the church of the

Badia, Orsanmichele, the Bargello and the Baptistry. In order to achieve a city that should be new but harmonious, one man, Arnolfo di Cambio, was given the responsibility of directing and coordinating the work. One of the greatest architects and sculptors of his time, he raised the level of the piazza (which he had re-paved), eliminating the podium on which the Baptistry previously stood, demolished a few houses nearby, and began to build the new cathedral, for which he planned a cupola and external decoration matching that of the Baptistry. The death of Arnolfo in 1302 put a stop to the work, which was resumed in 1332-34 with the construction of the Bell-Tower under the direction of Giotto. The addition of a cupola by Brunelleschi made it the impressive, dominating building that we see today (the façade is a 19th century work).

The interior of the Cathedral.

CATHEDRAL

The construction of the Cathedral, dedicated to Santa Maria del Fiore (St. Mary of the Flower) was begun in 1294 by Arnolfo di Cambio, chosen by the city authorities and the citizens, who wanted a cathedral not only larger than the previous church of Santa Reparata but also "so sumptuous and magnificent" that it would outdo the cathedrals of rival Tuscan cities both in beauty and dimensions. The new cathedral was erected round the older church, whose simple structure and two bell-towers were incorporated. Santa Reparata was finally pulled down in 1375; but the Florentines went on calling the new cathedral by the old name for a long time — the authorities had to inflict heavy fines in order to enforce the use of the new one, Santa Maria del Fiore. The lower part of Santa Reparata, buried underneath the floor of the Duomo till quite recently, can now be visited by going down a staircase from the right aisle; it contains remains of frescoes, sculptures and tombstones, including that of Filippo Brunelleschi. The inside of the Duomo,

solemn, spacious and light, was the scene of the fiery sermons of Savonarola, and of the savage Pazzi conspiracy. On April 26th 1478 members of the Pazzi family, enemies of the Medicis, in league with Archbishop Salviati, attacked Lorenzo the Magnificent and his brother Giuliano during Mass. Lorenzo escaped, but Giuliano was killed and the conspiracy was followed by harsh repression. Works of art of many centuries embellish the cathedral but do not alter the severity of its high ogival arches and composite pillars. On the inside of the façade is an enormous clock, executed in 1443 and decorated with four heads of *Prophets* painted by Paolo Uccello. Also by Paolo Uccello is the fresco of the *Monument to Giovanni Acuto* (John Hawkwood) on the wall in the left aisle; beside it is that of the *Monument to Niccolò da Tolentino*, by Andrea del Castagno (1456). Above the large octagonal tribune is the cupola by Brunelleschi. A competition for the construction of the cupola was announced in 1418. The difficulty of this task was immediately evident,

Above: *Monument to Niccolò da Tolentino, by Andrea del Castagno;* right: *Monument to Giovanni Acuto (John Hawkwood), by Paolo Uccello;* at the side: *Dante and the Divine Comedy, by Domenico di Michelino.*

Two views of the interior of the Cathedral.

The Crypt of Santa Reparata; below: *St. John (detail of a fresco with the Passion of Christ).*

for traditional building techniques were inadequate. Brunelleschi invented an original system of mobile centres which superseded the usual one of fixed structures starting from the ground (clearly impossible to use owing to the enormous dimensions of the building) and so succeeded in defeating Lorenzo Ghiberti, his eternal rival, who also took part in the competition. The cupola was closed up as far as the lantern in 1436. It is based on a massive octagonal drum, has marble ribbing and is covered by red tiles baked in the kilns at Impruneta. The inside of the cupola is decorated with frescoes by Giorgio Vasari and Federico Zuccari (1572-79) representing the *Last Judgment* in five superimposed bands. Over the high altar is a wooden *Crucifix* by Benedetto da Maiano; and round it is the octagonal choir by Baccio Bandinelli (1555), decorated with bas-reliefs. Behind the altar on the right is the Old Sacristy with an *Ascension* in terracotta by Luca della Robbia in the lunette over the entrance. Directly opposite on the other side of the Tribune is the New Sacristy, with a fine bronze door by Luca della Robbia, Michelozzo and Maso di Bartolomeo. In the lunette, *Resurrection*, also by Luca. Inside the sacristy, splendid 15th century inlaid cupboards. In the chapel at the end of the apse is a bronze urn by Ghiberti with relics of Saint Zanobius.

The dome of the Cathedral.

The Loggia del Bigallo; at the side: Giotto's Bell Tower.

LOGGIA DEL BIGALLO

This was built between 1352 and 1358 by Alberto Arnoldi in elegant Gothic style. The front, facing the Baptistry, has three tabernacles with the statues of *St. Peter the Martyr*, the *Virgin and Child* and *St. Luke*. Inside is a fine collection of works of art, with frescoes detached from the building and works by Ghirlandaio, Arnoldi and the schools of Botticelli and Verrocchio.

GIOTTO'S BELL TOWER

The building of this tower began in 1334 under the direction of Giotto, after a fire had destroyed the old bell-tower of Santa Reparata. Giotto died in 1337, when the base of the tower had been completed; after him work was directed by Andrea Pisano and Francesco Talenti, who brought it to conclusion (although the original plan included a spire which was never built). The building is of remarkable grace and elegance; the structure lightens and lengthens as it rises, becoming complex with marble insets and fine perforation. The bas-reliefs on the base (the originals are in the Cathedral Museum) were executed by Andrea Pisano and his workmen under the supervision of Giotto.

The Baptistry of San Giovanni; facing page: the South Door, by Andrea Pisano.

BAPTISTRY

Dante's "Bel San Giovanni", the religious building most beloved by the Florentines, was perhaps started in the 7th century, but the work done in the 11th-12th centuries made it the most important monument of Romanesque architecture in Florence. Its regular octagonal form and the symmetrical distribution of the external decoration were for centuries an architectural ideal for artists of the stature of Arnolfo, Giotto, Brunelleschi, Leon Battista Alberti, Leonardo and Michelangelo. It has three magnificent bronze doors. The South Door is the work of Andrea Pisano (c. 1330); it consists of 28 panels illustrating the *Life of the Baptist*; the

bronze cornice is the work of Vittorio Ghiberti (son of Lorenzo, 1452). The North Door is by Lorenzo Ghiberti, executed 1403-1424, after winning a competition against Brunelleschi; the 28 panels represent episodes from the *Life of Christ*. The East Door, the famous "door of Paradise", is also by Lorenzo Ghiberti (1425-1452); it is composed of 10 gilt panels, with complex *Scenes from the Old Testament*, crowded with figures. The smooth pyramidal roof-covering is topped by a lantern. The inside of the Baptistry, like the outside, is on an octagonal plan with marble panelling and each wall divided into three by tall columns; the two-lighted

Creation of Adam and Eve. – Original Sin. – Expulsion from Paradise.	Adam and Eve, Cain and Abel. – Abel keeping sheep and Cain ploughing. – Cain kills Abel. – Curse of Cain.
Story of Noah: Noah's family leaves the ark after the Flood. – Noah gives thanks to the Lord who sends a rainbow as a sign of peace. – Drunkenness of Noah. – Noah is derided by Ham and covered up by Shem and Japhet.	Story of Abraham: Sarah at the entrance to the tent. – Apparition of the angels to Abraham. – Abraham and Isaac on the mountain. – The Angel stays Abraham's hand as he is about to sacrifice Isaac.
Story of Jacob and Esau: Esau trades his birthright for a plate of lentils. – Isaac sends Esau hunting. – Jacob throws a goat's skin around his neck. – Isaac mistakes Jacob for Esau and gives him his blessing. – Jacob leaves his father's house.	Story of Joseph: Joseph is sold to the merchants and brought before Pharaoh. – Interpretation of Pharaoh's dream. – The golden cup in Benjamin's bag. – Joseph reveals himself to his brothers and forgives them. – Joseph meets Jacob.
Lorenzo Ghiberti	Vittorio Ghiberti
Story of Moses: Moses receives the Tablets of the Law on Mount Sinai. – Aaron waits halfway down the mountain. – The Hebrews, terrified by the thunder and lightning, await Moses' return at the foot of the mountain.	Story of Joshua: Joshua and the Hebrews cross the Jordan and crowd before the Ark. – The Hebrews gather twelve stones for commemoration. – The walls of Jericho fall at the sound of the Angels' trumpets.
Story of Saul and David: Saul defeats the Philistines. – David smites Goliath. – David carries Goliath's head before the cheering crowd, back to Jerusalem.	King Solomon ceremoniously receives the Queen of Sheba in the Temple of Jerusalem.

At the side, from top to bottom: *Lorenzo and Vittorio Ghiberti;* preceding page: *the Door of Paradise, by Lorenzo Ghiberti.*

windows of the women's gallery open above the trabeation. A baptismal font, mentioned by Dante in the *Divine Comedy,* used to stand in the centre of the very fine inlaid marble floor; this was removed in the 16th century by Buontalenti, by order of the Grand Duke Francesco I. Against the wall are a baptismal font of the Pisan school, 14th century; the tomb of the anti-Pope John XXIII, the work of Donatello and Michelozzo, commissioned by the banker Giovanni dei Medici, two Roman sarcophagi and a 13th century altar. The beautiful and very striking wooden statue of the *Magdalen* by Donatello (1435-55), which used to be in the Baptistry, is now on view in the Cathedral Museum. The internal sections of the cupola are covered by mosaics executed between the mid-13th and the mid-14th century by local and Venetian craftsmen (in the Middle Ages Venice was the greatest centre for mosaics). The most important artists who made the cartoons for the mosaics include Cimabue (*Scenes from the life of Joseph*) and Coppo di Marcovaldo (*Christ*). The subjects of the magnificent design are *Scenes from the Old and New Testament* and the *Last Judgment,* dominated by the impressive figure of the *Judging Christ,* more than twenty six feet high.

The interior of the cupola of the Baptistry.

The 13th and 14th-century mosaics that cover the cupola of the Baptistry are by artists of the Venetian and Florentine schools; the decoration, on a gold ground, is divided into concentric bands. In the centre, round the opening, of the lantern, are ornamental motifs; there follows the image of Christ surrounded by Seraph and the angelic host, in the thirt band are scenes from Genesis (from the Creation to the Flood), in the fourth, the story of Joseph, in the fifth, scenes of the Life of Christ and In the last, the life of the Baptist. The apsidal zone is dominated by the colossal figure of Christ: on either side, in three superimposed bands, are: Angels announcing judgement; the Virgin, the Baptist and Apostles; the Resurrection of the Dead and the division of the Blessed and the Damned, with a terrible representation of Hell.

The Room of the Choir-galleries; at the side: *Choir-gallery, by Luca della Robbia (detail).*

CATHEDRAL MUSEUM

This museum contains works from the Cathedral, the Bell-Tower and Baptistry. A room on the ground floor houses the sculptures from the first façade of the Cathedral, demolished in 1587, with a splendid *Virgin and Child* by Arnolfo di Cambio. The next room contains building material and mechanical devices used by Brunelleschi when building the Cupola. Another small room has a collection of precious reliquaries. The famous *Pietà* by Michelangelo is on the mezzanine. On the floor above, the two choir-galleries by Donatello and Luca della Robbia; *panels* by Andrea Pisano from the Bell-Tower, the statues of *John the Baptist*, the *Magdalen* and *Habakkuk* by Donatello, and the silver altar from the Baptistry, the work of several artists including Michelozzo, Verrocchio and Pollaiolo.

Three works by Donatello: Jeremiah (above), Ha-bakkuk (below) and The Magdalen (at the side).

Above: *two works by Arnolfo di Cambio*; left: *Madonna and Child*; right: *statue of Boniface VIII*; at the side: *the silver cross of the altar in the Baptistry, by Betto di Francesco, Antonio del Pollaiolo and Bernardino Cennini*; facing page: *The Pietà, by Michelangelo.*

ORSANMICHELE

The religious and civic centres of Florence, Piazza del Duomo and Piazza della Signoria, are connected by Via Calzaioli, an elegant, busy shopping street, in which stands the square mass of Orsanmichele, a building erected for civic use and subsequently converted into a church. In 1284 the Florentine republic appointed Arnolfo to build a loggia for the collection and storage of grain, in the garden (orto) of the Monastery of San Michele — hence the name. This was burnt down in 1304, and rebuilt between 1337 and 1404 by Francesco Talenti and Neri di Fioravante in the elegant and ornate "decorated" Gothic style. The stores were kept on the two upper floors, the grain came down to the loggia below, through the supporting pillars and flowed out at the openings provided. The external decoration was contracted out to the various city Guilds; each had a tabernacle with its coat of arms and the statue of its patron saint. Remarkable, among the sculptures, are: the *Baptist* and *St. Matthew* by Ghiberti, *St. George* by Donatello (original in the Bargello) and the classical *Four Crowned Saints* by Nanni di Banco. The interior has a double nave with high cross vaults; in the right one, *tabernacle* by Andrea Orcagna (1359), a large Gothic cusped shrine, whose base is decorated with bas-reliefs of *Scenes of the life of the Virgin* and which contains the *Madonna of the Graces*, by Bernardo Daddi (1347).

The exterior and the interior of Orsanmichele.

The Tabernacle, by Orcagna.

PIAZZA DELLA SIGNORIA

In Roman times, the area that is now the civic centre of the town was occupied by dwelling houses and the theatre. At the end of the 13th century the zone was included in the town-planning scheme directed by Arnolfo di Cambio, who requisitioned and pulled down the houses of Ghibelline families standing there and began to build Palazzo Vecchio. Henceforward the piazza became the setting for public speeches, ceremonies, meetings, uproars, executions: famous, especially, that of Gerolamo Savonarola, the preacher who was, for a short time, the arbiter of political life in the city, was excommunicated and burnt at the stake as a heretic on May 23rd, 1498, on the spot now indicated by a plaque. Now the piazza lacks unity owing to uncoordinated building around it, which went on until last century. The Gothic loggia was erected in the 14th century; a false Renaissance-style palace was built opposite Palazzo Vecchio in the nineteenth century. On the side opposite the Loggia, at N° 5, is the Alberto della Ragione collection (works of contemporary Italian art) and at N° 7, Palazzo Uguccioni, executed from a design by Michelangelo or Raphael, and on the other side the Tribunal of the Guilds (1359).

Tribunale di Mercatanzia (Merchants' Court); below, left: *Equestrian monument to Cosimo I dei Medici, by Giambologna.*

NEPTUNE FOUNTAIN

Bartolomeo Ammannati was employed by Grand Duke Cosimo I on the recommendation of Vasari. He worked as an architect on the rebuilding of the Pitti Palace, of the two bridges of Carraia and Santa Trinita, and on the building of many palaces in the city; as a sculptor, his most important work is this fountain in the piazza, commissioned by Cosimo and executed between 1563 and 1576. In the centre of the polygonal pool is the large figure of *Neptune* (a slight resemblance to Cosimo may indicate an intention to flatter him); beneath the statue is a coach drawn by sea-horses; all round and at the edge of the pool are the magnificent bronze figures of *Naiads, Tritons* and *Satyrs,* works that reveal the hand of Giambologna, who was Ammannati's assistant. The fountain has been damaged several times; one night during Carneval in 1830 a group of tipsy young men in masks bore off a Triton and threw it into the Arno; the statue was never recovered, and has been substituted by a copy. There are more statues on the steps of the Palace: the *Marzocco,* the lion symbolic of the Florentine republic, a copy of the original by Donatello (Bargello); a copy of Michelangelo's *David* (Gallery of the Accademia), brought here in 1504 to symbolise the liberty to which Florence aspired during the brief republican period; *Hercules and Cacus* by Bandinelli (1534) and two statuettes (perhaps Philemon and Baucis changed into plants) by De' Rossi and Bandinelli.

The Neptune Fountain, by Bartolomeo Ammanna-
ti; below: *two details of the fountain.*

The Loggia dei Lanzi; facing page, from left to right: *The Perseus, by Benvenuto Cellini; The Rape of the Sabin Women, by Giambologna.*

LOGGIA DEI LANZI

This is also called the Loggia della Signoria because it was built to hold the public ceremonies of the Signoria under cover; or also the Loggia dell'Orcagna from the name of the architect who, according to Vasari, designed it. These Lanzi were the Lanzichenecchi (Landesknechts), German mercenaries in the pay of Cosimo I, who were housed in the building for a certain period. The Loggia was built between 1376 and 1383 by Benci di Cione and Simone Talenti. It consists of three large classical arches, on columns of different styles, leading to a large cross-vaulted porch. The lobed panels between the arches were executed between 1384 and 1389 from designs by Agnolo Gaddi and enclose statues of the *Virtues*. Piazza della Signoria became the scene of official functions and had to be a worthy setting for a state aspiring to be a Great Power; it was enriched with sculptures and the Loggia be-

came a sort of open-air public museum. Two heraldic *lions* flank the entrance: the one on the right is of the classical epoch, the other is sixteenth century. Under the right arch is the *Rape of the Sabine Women*, by Giambologna (1583); a work of refined virtuosity, which is a prelude to Baroque. The left arch frames the *Perseus* of Benvenuto Cellini (1546-54): the hero defeating the Medusa has the monumentality of Michelangelo together with the extenuated preciosity of contemporary Mannerism; the base is splendid, with statues and bas-reliefs that reveal the artist's skill as a goldsmith. Cellini was only able to complete the statue after solving many technical problems, and after ten years of entreaty to Cosimo to allow him the honour of sculpting something for Piazza Signoria. The loggia also contains *Hercules and Nessus*, another group by Giambologna, *Menelaus bearing the body of Patrocles*, a Roman copy of a Greek original of the 4th century B.C.; six Roman female statues and the *Rape of Polixena*, a fine work by Pio Fedi.

the Republican authorities, the Priors and the Standard-bearer harangued the populace; this was removed in the last century. The interior of the palace is of the greatest interest both for the rooms themselves and the works of art. On the ground floor the fine courtyard by Michelozzo and the Arms Hall (entrance on the left side of the palace, opened only for temporary exhibitions); austere and bare, it is the only fourteenth century room that has been left unaltered, and is interesting on that account. On the first floor, the magnificent Hall of the Five Hundred, with the adjacent Study of Francesco I, the Hall of the Two Hundred by the brothers Da Maiano (1472-77) with a fine coffered ceiling in wood (this housed the Council of two hundred citizens who discussed wars and alliances, and is now used by the Borough Council); the apartments of Leo X, with a chapel and rooms frescoed with *Scenes of the Medici family* by Vasari and helpers (only the rooms of Leo X, Lorenzo the Magnificent and Cosimo I can be visited because the others are occupied by the Mayor and aldermen). On the second floor, the Apartment of the Elements, designed by Giovanni Battista del Tasso (c. 1550). These rooms too were decorated by Vasari and helpers,

On this and the facing page: *views of Piazza della Signoria and Palazzo Vecchio.*

PALAZZO VECCHIO

Palazzo della Signoria, called Palazzo Vecchio, the old palace, after the middle of the 15th century when the Medicis left it and moved to Palazzo Pitti, was the residence of the highest authorities in the city, her political centre, (the Borough council is still housed there) and a symbol of the strength and harmony of established institutions. The building was begun in 1299 and was probably designed by the great architect Arnolfo di Cambio. The original edifice, a massive rusticated cube three storeys high, graced with fine two-lighted windows, is crowned by a gallery projecting on brackets, above which soars the beautiful and mighty tower; under the arches, between the brackets, are repeated the nine coats of arms of the Comune of Florence, including the best known, a red lily on a white ground. Some of the brackets have trap doors (machicolations) from which, in the not infrequent case of risings or revolts, stones, boiling oil and molten lead were thrown at assailants. The tower, 94 metres high, is, by a stroke of genius, placed off-centre, to echo the asymmetry of the piazza; it was finished in 1310. The palace was repeatedly enlarged, in 1343, in 1495 (by Cronaca) and in the 16th century by Vasari, who considerably altered the interior, by Giovanni Battista del Tasso and by Buontalenti. In 1323 a high balustrade was built on the two sides overlooking the piazza, from which

some with fine inlaid cabinets, and also the lovely Saturn Terrace with its splendid view; the Apartments of Eleonora di Toledo, wife of Cosimo I, where special mention should be made of the Gualdrada room, with another fine cabinet, in ebony and hard precious stones, and the chapel, entirely frescoed by Bronzino, who also painted the very fine altar-piece (*Pietà*, 1553); the chapel of the Signoria; the very fine Audience Hall, with coffered ceiling and marble doorway, both by Benedetto da Maiano, which contains a beautiful wooden bench designed by Vasari, the famous, dramatic bronze group by Donatello representing *Judith and Holofernes* (c. 1455) formerly on the steps in front of the palace; the magnificent and sumptuous Lily room with the Map room and the Chancery next to it; Machiavelli, of whom there is a coloured clay bust and a portrait here, worked in this room for several years as the Secretary of the Republic; and here is the original of the charming fountain in the courtyard, *Boy with a Dolphin*, by Verrocchio (1476). On the mezzanine (reached from the Apartment of the Elements) is a series of 15 rooms containing an important collection of works of art recovered in Germany after World War II. Among the most remarkable things are the so-called *Lancellotti Discobolus*, the best Roman copy of the famous Miro Discobolus, (Greek, 5th century B.C.) which has disappeared, like almost all the Greek originals; the *Crouching Aphrodite*, Roman sculpture, 2nd century A.D.; two fine

The entrance portico of Palazzo Vecchio; below: *Courtyard, by Michelozzo.*

The Hall of the Five Hundred; below: *Victory over the Pisans at Torre San Vincenzo, a fresco by Vasari.*

coloured panels in *opus sectile*, 331 A.D.; Greek and Roman reliefs and sculptures of various epochs. Of medieval and modern art: a beautiful little painting on wood of the *Madonna of Humility* attributed to Masolino and another very small one attributed to Masaccio; a large *Nativity* by Antoniazzo Romano; *Pygmalion and Galathea* by Bronzino; a fragment, barely rough-hewn but very fine, of the *Rondanini Pietà* by Michelangelo; *Venus and Mercury present their son Anteros to Jove*, by Paolo Veronese; *Leda and the Swan*, by Tintoretto; *Portrait of Elizabeth of Valois*, by Coelho; *Judith with the head of Holofernes* and a large *Equestrian portrait of Giovanni Carlo Doria* by Rubens; a beautiful *Portrait of an Unknown Man* by Hans Memling; the *Ecstasy of St. Cecilia* by Bernardo Cavallino; an exquisite *Portrait of Felicita Sartori* by Rosalba Carriera; Venetian landscapes attributed to Francesco Guardi and the circle of Canaletto; and lastly the pathetic *Maternity* by the nineteenth century German painter Friedrich von Amerling. Also on the mezzanine are the Museum of Musical instruments, containing rare and antique instruments of various periods, and the Loeser Collection, an important legacy of sculptures and paintings by Tuscan artists from the 14th to the 16th century. The most important works are: in sculpture, two terracotta groups representing soldiers and knights, by Giovan Fracesco Rustici (16th

Hercules and Cacus, by Vincenzo de' Rossi; below, left: *Hercules and Diomedes, by Vincenzo de' Rossi*; right: *Victory, by Michelangelo*; facing page: *Study of Francesco I dei Medici.*

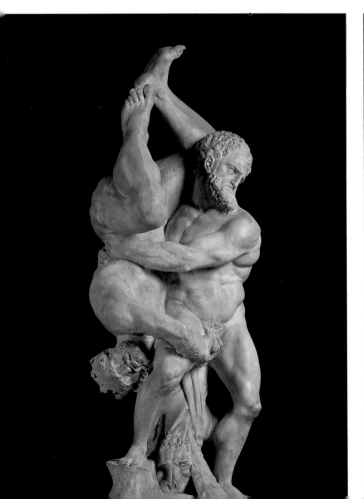

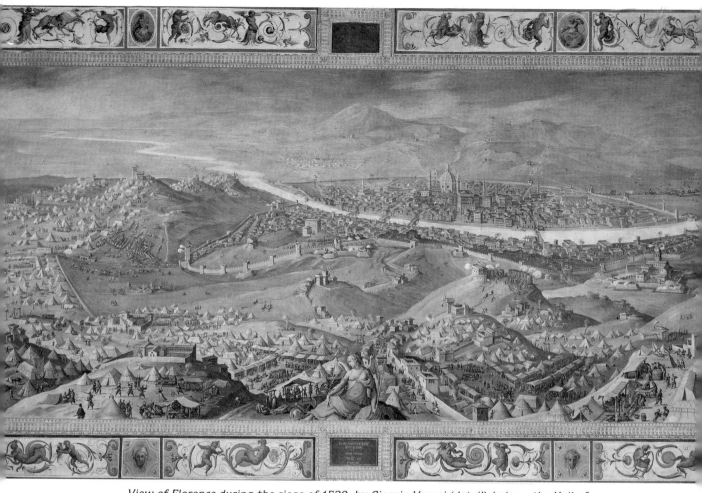

View of Florence during the siege of 1530, by Giorgio Vasari (detail); below: *the Hall of Leo X.*

The Lily Room; at the side: Judith and Holofernes, by Donatello.

century); a splendid *Madonna and Child*, in painted wood, attributed to the school of Arnolfo di Cambio and a marble *Angel* by Tino di Camaino; in painting: the *Passion of Christ*, a curious work by Piero di Cosimo, end of 15th century: "an abstract and original spirit", Vasari called him in his *Life*; a *Virgin and Child* by Pietro Lorenzetti (first half of 14th century) and the remarkable *Portrait of Laura Battiferri* (wife of the sculptor Ammannati) by Agnolo Bronzino.

Piazzale degli Uffizi at night.

UFFIZI GALLERY

The Uffizi is not only the oldest art gallery in the world; it is the most important in Italy and also one of the greatest in Europe and in the whole world, visited by more than a million people every year. The gallery owns about 4800 works, of which about 2000 are on view (1000 paintings, 300 sculptures, 46 tapestries, 14 pieces of furniture and pottery, besides 700 more paintings kept in the Vasari corridor); the rest is in storage or on loan to other museums. This enormous quantity of works includes countless masterpieces, some being among the highest achievements of Western art. The building containing the Gallery is itself splendid; it was built for Cosimo I in the mid 16th century in the zone between Palazzo Vecchio and the Arno, to house the public offices (hence the name); the 11th century church of San Pietro Scheraggio, and the old Mint, where florins were coined, were partly

The Loggia of the Uffizi overlooking the Arno; below: *view of the first corridor.*

Above: *Madonna in Majesty*, by Duccio di Buoninsegna; above, left: *Madonna in Majesty*, by Giotto; at the side: *Annunciation*, by Simone Martini; *Saint Ansano and Giulitta*, at the sides, are by Lippo Memmi.

incorporated. The planning was entrusted to Giorgio Vasari, a great and eclectic figure in art at the time, court painter and architect, writer on art (his *Lives of the most excellent architects, sculptors and painters* is the most important source for the study of the history of Italian art) who built it between 1559 and the year of his death (and that of Cosimo), 1574; the building, highly original, is erected over two long porticoes joined by a third side that opens on to the Arno with a magnificent arch of great scenic effect. The outside of the Uffizi is inspired by the style of Michelangelo's vestibule for the Laurentian Library, also with ribbing in pietra serena on white plaster. Together with the marvellous Corridor, it is certainly Vasari's masterpiece in architecture. Work on the Uffizi was resumed in 1580, by order of Francesco I, and directed by Bernardo Buontalenti, who built the large Medici Theatre (dismantled in 1890) and the famous Tribune; at the same time the top storey of the loggia was rebuilt, the offices were transferred elsewhere and some of the rooms were used for collections of works of art, arms, and scientific curiosities; and so the Gallery was born. The first nucleus of works already included paintings by Botticelli, Lippi, Paolo Uccello; about 1600 Ferdinando I had all the works at the Villa Medici in Rome transferred to the Uffizi; in 1631 Ferdinando II contributed an important collection of paintings, (originally in Urbino, the inher-

At the side: *Presentation of Jesus in the Temple, by Ambrogio Lorenzetti*; below: *The Battle of San Romano, by Paolo Uccello.*

Above: *two works by Piero della Francesca*; left: *Portrait of Battista Sforza*; right: *Portrait of Federico da Montefeltro*; at the side: *Crucifix with the Magdalen, by Luca Signorelli*; facing page: *Madonna and Child with Two Angels, by Filippo Lippi.*

itance of his wife Vittoria della Rovere) including works by Piero della Francesca, Titian and Raphael; at the end of the 17th century Cosimo III collected gems, medals and coins and brought the *Venus*, later known as the "Medici" Venus, and other important antique sculptures from Rome; Anna Maria Ludovica, Electress Palatine, the last heir to the Medicis, enlarged the collection with Flemish and German paintings and left it in its entirety to the state of Tuscany in her will (1743). The Lorraines also helped to enlarge the gallery's artistic patrimony and Pietro Leopoldo (2nd half of the 18th century) reorganised it, appointed a Director, and rearranged everything. In the nineteenth century, owing to the pillage of the Napoleonic wars, which was only restored in part, and above all to the creation of new specialised museums (Archaeological Museum, Bargello, Fra Angelico Museum, Science Museums, Silver Museum etc.) many works were removed from the Uffizi and it became what it is today. Extensive restoration of many of the works has been effected since the second world war, and is still in progress.

Above: *Hercules and the Hydra, by Antonio del Pollaiolo;* above, left: *Coronation of the Virgin, by Sandro Botticelli;* at the side: *Adoration of the Magi, by Domenico Ghirlandaio;* facing page: *Portrait of a Young Man with a Medal depicting Cosimo the Elder, by Sandro Botticelli.*

Holy Family with the Infant Saint John, by Michelangelo; preceding page: *two works by Sandro Botticelli*; above: *Spring or Primavera*; below: *The Birth of Venus*.

Above: *Annunciation, by Leonardo da Vinci*; at the side: *Flora, by Titian*; facing page, above, left to right: *Portrait of Benedetto Portinari, by Hans Memling; Sts. John Evangelist and Francis, by Domenico Theotokòpulos*, known as *El Greco*; below: *Death of Adonis, by Sebastiano del Piombo*.

THE DRAWINGS AND PRINTS COLLECTION

This collection of drawings and prints, now one of the greatest in the world, was begun by Cardinal Leopoldo dei Medici in the 17th century; when he died (1675) the material was brought from Pitti Palace to the Uffizi and was rearranged by Filippo Baldinucci, a scholar commissioned to do this by Cosimo III; it already amounted to about 100 volumes. The collection was then increased by legacies and purchases, and today reaches the considerable figure of more than 50,000 drawings and 60,000 prints by all the major Italian and foreign artists (only a few of them modern); these include Paolo Uccello, Fra Angelico, Botticelli, Leonardo, Michelangelo, Raphael, Brueghel, Dürer, Lorrain and countless others. The rooms are on the first floor of the Uffizi in the place of the former Medici Theatre, built by Buontalenti in 1585 for court festivities, balls and plays, and are reached by going up the magnificent staircase designed by Vasari. The large theatre, the first of the modern epoch, occupied most of this wing of the building and saw the birth of Melodrama (early 17th century). Application must be made to visit the Drawing and Print rooms which are only accessible to students: the first room is used for temporary exhibitions.

At the side: *Study for Pallas, by Sandro Botticelli;* below: *two works by Leonardo da Vinci;* left: *Study of two heads;* right: *Landscape Study (detail);* facing page: *Study of a man's head, by Michelangelo.*

VASARI CORRIDOR

Conceived as a passage by air from the Grand Ducal Palace, Pitti, to the seat of government (the Uffizi), and, along another short passage, to Palazzo Vecchio, this singular feat of architecture and town planning was executed in the short space of five months, in 1565, by Giorgio Vasari, commissioned by Cosimo I. The Vasari Corridor starts from the Uffizi on the third floor between Room XXV and Room XXXIV, runs along the Arno over an arcade, crosses the river over Ponte Vecchio, passes between houses and palaces on the other side of the river, along beside the façade of the church of Santa Felicita (the Grand Dukes attended religious services there, unseen in a private box); it continues along the side of Boboli Garden and, after a distance of nearly a kilometre, enters the Pitti Palace. It was damaged in World War II and only reopened in 1973. About seven hundred paintings are on view, including seventeenth and eighteenth century Italian works, portraits of the Medicis and the Lorraines, and above all the famous collection of self-portraits, the most complete in the world, extending from the fourteenth century to the present time, including nearly all the greater Italian artists and numerous foreign ones.

Self-portrait, by Diego Velazquez; below, from left to right: *Self-portrait, by Jacques Louis David; Self-portrait, by Eugène Delacroix.*

PIAZZA SAN FIRENZE

Not far from Piazza della Signoria, and not very large, this piazza is dominated by two fine, large palaces of different epoch and style. One of these is Palazzo Gondi, by Giuliano da Sangallo (1490-1501). Opposite is the great building of the so-called San Firenze, the best Baroque in Florence, (end of 17th and 18th century). Now the seat of the Tribunal, it incorporates the church of San Filippo Neri, known as San Firenze, with a fine interior, also Baroque.

NATIONAL MUSEUM (BARGELLO)

This is the most important Italian museum of sculpture and minor arts. It is housed in the severe square Bargello palace, a 13th century building of great historical importance, that was begun in 1255 and was first used as the seat of the Captain of the People. After 1574 it was the seat of the Captain of Justice, called the Bargello (that is the chief of police) and the palace became grimly famous for the

Palazzo del Bargello; below: *the courtyard of the palace.*

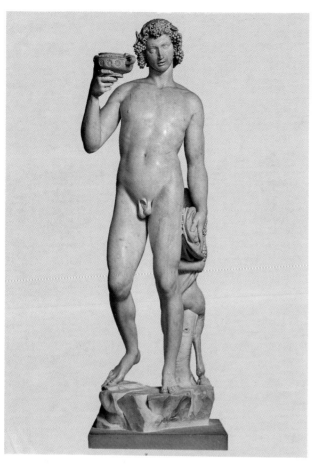

executions held there; condemned men who escaped capture were hanged in effigy, that is, portraits of them, hanging head downwards, were painted on the city walls; painters engaged on this job included Botticelli, Andrea del Sarto and Andrea del Castagno, known by his contemporaries as Andrea degli Impiccati (Hanged men). The Museum was founded in 1865. A description of the principal works must begin with the splendid courtyard, where, under the arches, is, among other things, a large and very fine cannon of the early 17th century and, among the sculptures, the delightful *Fisherman* by Vincenzo Gemito (1877). One of the rooms on the ground floor contains masterpieces by Michelangelo such as the bust of *Brutus* (c. 1540), who was seen at that time as a heroic liberator from tyranny; the so-called *Pitti tondo* (c. 1504), rendered with the characteristic and expressive "unfinished" style; the *David-Apollo* (c. 1531), delicate and harmonious; the youthful *Drunken Bacchus* (1497-99); among other works, another *Bacchus* by Sansovino (1520) and the bronze bust of *Cosimo I*, by Benvenuto Cellini (1546-57). On the first floor, on the fine balcony are more bronzes by Giambologna, including the famous *Mercury*; in the Donatello Hall,

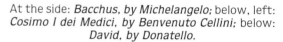

At the side: *Bacchus, by Michelangelo;* below, left: *Cosimo I dei Medici, by Benvenuto Cellini;* below: *David, by Donatello.*

Brutus, by Michelangelo; at the side: *David, by Donatello.*

besides masterpieces by the great 15th century sculptor, are numerous terracottas by Luca della Robbia and the panels with the *Sacrifice of Isaac* by Brunelleschi and Ghiberti; in the other rooms, splendid majolicas from Faenza and other factories, enamels, goldsmiths' work, liturgical objects, ivories of various periods. On the second floor: a room with terracottas by Giovanni della Robbia and one with those of Andrea della Robbia; a room devoted to Verrocchio, that also contains works by Rossellino, Pollaiolo and others; lastly, two rooms with the collections of small bronzes and of arms.

At the side: *Madonna and Child with the Infant Saint John, by Michelangelo, known as the "Pitti Tondo"*; below, left: *Narcissus, by Benvenuto Cellini*; below: *Idealized Portrait of a Boy, by Andrea della Robbia*; facing page: *David, by Verrocchio.*

The church of Santa Croce on the square of the
same name; at the side: *Monument to Dante
Alighieri, by Enrico Pazzi*; facing page: *the facade
of Santa Croce.*

PIAZZA SANTA CROCE

From the Middle Ages onwards this piazza was the
scene of festivities, tournaments, meetings, games;
there was a famous tournament here between
Lorenzo and Giuliano dei Medici, St. Bernardino da
Siena preached here, the Florentine Carnival took
place here, like the game of football in Renaissance
costume. In 1865 Enrico Pazzi placed the monument
to Dante (later transferred to the front of the
church) in the middle of the square. On the south
side of the piazza is Palazzo dell'Antella, whose
façade, resting on corbels, was frescoed in the space
of three weeks by twenty painters directed by
Giuliano da Sangallo (17th century); on the door is a
bust of Cosimo II; between two windows on the
ground floor is a 16th century marble disc that
indicated the central line of the piazza for the
football game.

The interior of Santa Croce.

SANTA CROCE

This church originated as a small oratory, built here by a community of monks in 1228. In 1294 Arnolfo di Cambio began the construction of the present basilica, in the monumental but simple form, sober in decoration, that characterises Franciscan churches. Santa Croce was for the Franciscans what Santa Maria Novella, on the other side of the town, was for the Dominicans, the shrine, the core of the order in Florence, the temple par excellence. The church was consecrated in 1443 in the presence of Pope Eugene IV. In 1566 Giorgio Vasari was commissioned by Cosimo I to execute some altars in the side aisles; this involved destroying the old choir and numerous frescoes. The façade of the church was only executed in the mid 19th century from a design by Niccolò Matas, in a neo-Gothic style like the bell-tower, by Gaetano Baccani (1847). The extraordinary importance of this church, with its numerous works of art, is enhanced by the many tombs of illustrious men. The interior has a nave and two side aisles, with pointed arches resting on octagonal stone pillars. The floor contains no fewer than 276 tombstones, the oldest being 14th century. In the central nave, at the third pillar on the right, is the fine pulpit by Benedetto da Maiano (1472-76); the decorative panels in relief have *Stories of St. Francis*. In the right aisle, at the first pillar, the *Madonna of the Milk* by Rossellino (1478); opposite, the funeral monument to Michelangelo by Vasari and helpers (1570); the sculptures are allegories of Painting, Sculpture and Architecture. There are also the Cenotaph of Dante Alighieri (buried at Ravenna) by Stefano Ricci (1829); the tomb of Vittorio Alfieri, executed by Canova in 1810; that of Niccolò Machiavelli, by Spinazzi (1787); the splendid *Annunciation* by Donatello (c. 1435); the monument to Leonardo Bruni, by Rossellino (c. 1444); the tombs of Gioacchino Rossini and Ugo Foscolo. In the right transept, on the right, is the Castellani chapel, frescoed about 1385 by Agnolo Gaddi with *Stories of St. Nicholas of Bari*, *John the Baptist*, and *Anthony Abbot*. At the end of the transept is the entrance to the Baroncelli Chapel, frescoed with *Stories of the Virgin* by Taddeo Gaddi; on the altar a polyptych with the *Coronation of the Virgin*, from the workshop of Giotto. At the corner of the transept is the entrance to the fine 14th century Sacristy; on the right wall, three episodes from the *Passion* by Taddeo Gaddi and others; in the end wall is the entrance to the Rinuccini Chapel, with frescoes by Giovanni da Milano. Returning to the church one should visit the series of chapels along the end; the Peruzzi Chapel (fourth from the right) has splendid frescoes by Giotto with *Stories of the Baptist* and *St. John the Evangelist*; the Bardi Chapel (the fifth) has *Stories of St. Francis*, also by Giotto; this cycle is to be placed among the painter's masterpieces (c. 1325); the Chapel of the High Altar has frescoes by Agnolo Gaddi and a polyptych by Niccolò Gerini (end of 14th century). Of the end chapels on the left, the Bardi di Vernio Chapel has fine *Stories of St. Sylvester*, by Maso di Banco (c. 1340). The Bardi Chapel at the end of the transept has a *Crucifix* by Donatello (c. 1425). On the left, the Salviati Chapel with the 19th century tomb of Sofia Zamoyski by Lorenzo Bartolini. In the left aisle, another series of funeral monuments; among others, the tomb of Galileo Galilei by Giulio Foggini (18th century).

Cenotaph to Dante Alighieri, by Stefano Ricci; below, from left to right: *Monument to Galileo Galilei, by Giulio Foggini*; *Tomb of Michelangelo, designed by Vasari.*

At the side: *the Sacristy with the frescoes by Taddeo Gaddi, Spinello Aretino and Niccolò Gerini;* below, left to right: *Crucifixion, by Taddeo Gaddi; Madonna and Child with Saints, by Giovanni del Biondo, on the altar of the Rinuccini Chapel.* Preceding page, above, left: *the Bardi Chapel and the Peruzzi Chapel;* right: *Saint Francis and Events from his Life,* anonymous Florentine artist; below: *The Funeral of Saint Francis, by Giotto, in the Bardi Chapel.*

The entrance portico of the Pazzi Chapel.

PAZZI CHAPEL

On the right of the church of Santa Croce are the buildings of the Franciscan monastery. The first Cloister is against the wall of the right aisle; the porticoes are 14th-15th century; on the right of the entrance is the monument to Florence Nightingale, (1820-1910), the heroic "Lady of the Lamp" who anticipated the work of the Red Cross on the battlefields and in the field hospitals during the Crimean War. At the end of the cloister appears the wonderful front of the Pazzi chapel. Filippo Brunelleschi designed the building and began it (it had the function of chapterhouse of the monastery and family burial chapel for the commissioners) about 1430; he worked on it at intervals until 1444, then other architects completed the building. A pronaos precedes the entrance; this has six Corinthian co-lumns and a wide central arch; the frieze with *heads of cherubs* is by Desiderio da Settignano. The chapel has a cupola with conical covering (1461) and under the portico is another small cupola in coloured terracotta, by Luca della Robbia; by the same, the Tondo of St. Andrew over the door, the panels of which are splendidly carved by Giuliano da Maiano (1472). The rectangular interior has the geometrical limpidity and measured rhythm of the best creations of Brunelleschi: white walls, grooved pilaster strips in pietra serena, wide arches; the only touches of colour are the fine tondi by Luca della Robbia, with figures of *Apostles* and *Evangelists*. In the presbytery, a stained glass panel attributed to Alesso Baldovinetti and a small cupola with Signs of the Zodiac. Going out into the First Cloister, a doorway on the left leads into the Large Cloister, designed by Brunelleschi.

SANTA CROCE MUSEUM

This is housed in some of the rooms of the Monastery of Santa Croce. The first, and most important of these is the old 14th century Refectory; the end wall is covered by an enormous fresco by Taddeo Gaddi representing the *Tree of Life*, the *Last Supper* and other scenes; on the right wall is the grandiose *Crucifix* painted on wood by Cimabue, badly damaged by the flooding in 1966, and three fragments of the *Triumph of Death* frescoed by Orcagna on the walls of Santa Croce (they were found under Vasari's altars, and detached); on the left is the *St. Ludovic* in bronze by Donatello (1423). The remains of fourteenth and fifteenth century glass windows, the work of Andrea del Castagno, Agnolo Bronzino, Giorgio Vasari and others, are kept in the other rooms.

At the side: *Saint Louis, bronze statue, by Donatello;* below: *Crucifix, by Cimabue;* below, right: *Della Robbia tabernacle.*

Interior of the Synagogue; preceding page: *the facade.*

THE SYNAGOGUE

This marvellous temple, so prized by the Jewish community of Florence, was commenced in 1874 and was designed by the architects Treves, Falcini and Micheli. It was inaugurated on the 24th October 1882. The construction of the monumental building was financed by a conspicuous fund bequeathed by David Levi, who had been the chairman of the Board of the Israelitic University of Florence from 1860 to 1870. The building is in pure Moorish style. The interior is completely frescoed, while the Ehal is covered with gleaming Venetian mosaic. Due to the predominatly Levantine Jewish origin of the Florentine community, the official rite is orthodox Sephardic, whilst the Ashkenazi minority meets in a room next-door to the Temple. The Synagogue was much damaged during the IInd World War and suffered further during the 1966 flood. The restoration has been carried out thanks to the contributions of the many visitors who daily flock to the Temple from all over the world.

Ponte Vecchio; below: *Bust of Benvenuto Cellini, by Romanelli.*

PONTE VECCHIO

As the name implies, (Old Bridge), the oldest bridge in Florence: it has, in fact, existed since the time of the Roman colony, when the piers were of stone and the roadway of wood; destroyed by flooding in 1117 it was completely rebuilt in stone but collapsed again in the terrible flood of November 4th 1333; it was rebuilt for the last time in 1345 (perhaps by the painter-architect Taddeo Gaddi) with three spans, very wide, planned with room for shops on either side. First of all the butchers settled there (but later also grocers, smiths, shoemakers etc.); these built the characteristic back shops projecting over the river, resting on supports and brackets. However, in 1591 Ferdinando I evicted them all to concede the shops to the goldsmiths only; and since then the bridge has been almost like a single shop window full of precious stones, interrupted only by two squares in the middle; the one looking downstream has a bust of Benvenuto Cellini, "master of the goldsmiths" by Raffaello Romanelli (1900). On November 4th 1966 the latest, dramatic flooding of Florence put the bridge to the test again: the structure itself stood up well, but the fury of the waters burst through the goldsmiths' shops at the back and swept away quantities of jewels.

A view of Ponte Vecchio with the shops of the goldsmiths; below: *the Mannelli Tower.*

Pitti Palace; at the side: *the interior courtyard of the palace, by Bartolomeo Ammannati.*

PITTI PALACE

By the middle of the 15th century power was practically in the hands of the Medici family; Cosimo the Elder governed Florence from his new palace in Via Larga; Luca Pitti now led the faction that was most hostile to him and to his son Piero. Luca thought it was very important that he should own a palace finer than the one that Michelozzo was building for the Medicis. He chose the site, on the hill of Boboli, and commissioned Brunelleschi to design a building with windows as large as the doorways of the Medici palace and dimensions such that this would have fitted into his courtyard. Brunelleschi accepted with alacrity and produced the plans about 1445. Work began in 1457 (after the master's death) under the direction of Luca Fancelli, Brunelleschi's pupil. The façade overlooking the piazza consisted only of the seven central windows; it was of three storeys separated by slender balconies and covered with rusticated stone. At the death of Luca Pitti in 1473 the palace was still incomplete; then the Pitti family fell into disfavour, and work on it was begun again by the Medicis themselves, that is by Eleonora di Toledo, the wife of Cosimo I, who bought the building and the land behind it in 1549. In the 16th and 17th century this became the palace of the Medicis, who enlarged it, created a garden on the Boboli hill, lengthened the building to nine windows each side, employing Giulio and Alfonso Parigi, and decorated the interior sumptuously. In the 18th century Ruggieri and Poccianti built the two-porticoed side wings that enclose the piazza. The remarkable fact is that each successive enlargement substantially respected the original design by Brunelleschi. During the period in which Florence was the capital of Italy (1865-71) the palace was the residence of Vittorio Emanuele II. Since 1919 it has been the property of the Italian State. There are seven museums here: the Palatine Gallery, the Royal Apartments, the Silver Museum, the Gallery of Modern Art, the Gallery of Costume, the Coach Museum and the Porcelain Museum.

Marble relief; below: *The Artichoke Fountain, by Francesco del Tadda.*

The Madonna of the Chair, by Raphael.

PALATINE GALLERY

The Palatine Gallery has its own particular character: it is not an organic collection systematically arranged to present a "comprehensive review" of the art of a certain period or periods (like the Uffizi); it is, rather, a typical 17th century picture gallery that reflects the taste of its creator and hence of contemporary fashion; even the arrangement of the pictures manifests a decorative intention alien to the museographical criteria of today. This is, in fact, the charm of the Palatine Gallery, a "private"

museum, almost a home, with its elegant furniture, ornaments, ebony cabinets, inlaid tables, stuccoes, tapestries and fine cornices. The idea of this collection goes back to two of the last Medicis, Cosimo II and Ferdinando II, who commissioned a great Baroque decorator, Pietro da Cortona, to fresco some of the rooms on the first floor of the Pitti Palace with allegorical mythological subjects celebrating the glories of the house of Medici (1641-47); he began to arrange pictures in these rooms, creating a

Three works by Raphael; above: *The Grand-ducal Madonna;* above, right: *Portrait of Agnolo Doni;* at the side: *Ezechiel's Vision.*

Three works by Andrea del Sarto; above: The Assumption of the Virgin with Apostles and Saints; above, left: Madonna in Glory and Four Saints; at the side: Holy Family; facing page: The Veiled Woman, by Raphael.

new family collection to complement that already existing in the Uffizi. The Lorraines continued both with the decoration of the rooms and the collection of works of art; in 1828 Grand Duke Pietro Leopoldo opened the museum to the public, a liberal gesture quite in the spirit of the new European tendency towards a greater diffusion of culture. Limited at first to the fine rooms of Venus, Apollo, Mars, Jupiter and Saturn, the collection grew to its present dimensions until 1928, when a great number of paintings were exchanged with the Uffizi and many 16th and 17th century works were acquired.

Madonna and Child with the Infant Saint John, by Sandro Botticelli; at the side: Portrait of a Lady, by Sandro Botticelli; below: Concert, by Titian.

Events from the Life of Joseph Hebrew, by Andrea del Sarto.

At the side: *The Three Ages of Man,
Venetian school*; below, left: *The Magdalen, by Titian*; below: *Saint Jerome,
attributed to Piero del Pollaiolo.*

The Dining Room, decorated by Terreni and Castagnoli; at the side: The Throne Room.

ROYAL APARTMENTS

This is the name given to a series of richly decorated rooms on the first floor, formerly the residence of the rulers of the houses of Medici, Lorraine and Savoy. As a matter of fact the only ones who lived there permanently were the Medicis, from Cosimo I to Gian Gastone (died 1737) who used to stay in bed the whole time, governing the state, eating, or receiving guests or mistresses. He was succeeded by his sister Anna Maria Ludovica, who left the Grand Duchy to the Lorraine family. The Lorraines preferred to live in the Villa of Poggio Imperiale, while the Savoy family had a liking for the Villa della Petraia, at Castello. The most interesting rooms are: the Green Room with 18th century Gobelin tapestries and a large 17th century cabinet; the Throne Room; the Chapel; the Parrot Room, the first of those forming the Apartments of Queen Margherita; the Yellow Room; the Queen's boudoir with oriental style decorations; the Apartment of Umberto I with fine portraits and furnishings; the Bona Room with frescoes by Poccetti, and the neoclassical White Room, the large and luminous palace ballroom, where temporary exhibitions are now frequently held.

Three examples of the art of the German goldsmiths from the jewellery collection of the Palatine Electress: Rooster, Fisherman and the Siren.

SILVER MUSEUM

This was instituted in 1919 and arranged on the ground floor of Pitti Palace, in the rooms that were used as the summer apartments of the Grand Dukes. Among the most interesting of these, from the point of view of decoration, are the Room of Giovanni da San Giovanni and the three successive ones, frescoed by Colonna and Mitelli between 1638 and 1644. The collection includes goldsmiths' work, enamels, cameos, crystal and work in hard stones collected by the Medicis and the Lorraines. Among the most important pieces are: vases in hard stones belonging to the Magnificent; 17th century German ivories; vase in lapis lazuli by Buontalenti (1583): the jewels of the bishop-princes of Salzburg; drinking cup belonging to Diane de Poitiers (16th century); relief of *Cosimo II in prayer*, (17th century).

Above: *Portrait of Madame Trentanove, by Vittorio Corcos*; above, right: *Portrait of the Daughter of Jack la Bolina, by Vittorio Corcos*; at the side: *The Dance, by Giovanni Bastianini*.

GALLERY OF MODERN ART

This contains a representative collection of 19th century painting, especially Tuscan. The first group of rooms is devoted to neo-classical and romantic works: a *Head of Calliope* by Canova; *Hercules at the crossroads* by Pompeo Batoni, the *Battle of Legnano* by Cassioli, works by Benvenuti, Dupré and Bezzuoli. In the second group are paintings of the second half of the century, with particular emphasis on the Macchiaioli, the most important current in Italian art at that time; the *Man caught by the stirrup*, the *Cavalry Charge* and the *Palmieri Rotunda* by Giovanni Fattori; works by Lega, Corcos and Signorini, and lastly paintings by Elisabeth Chaplin, Previati, Medardo Rosso and Vermehren.

The Amphitheatre; at the side: *The Bacchus Fountain, by Valerio Cioli.*

BOBOLI GARDEN

The creation of a garden on the hill at Boboli began at the same time as the rebuilding of the Pitti Palace for Cosimo I and Eleonora di Toledo at about the middle of the 16th century. Niccolò Pericoli, called 'Il Tribolo', architect and sculptor, had the job of laying out the large area to make it harmonize with the palace, according to the new Renaissance (and later Baroque) conception of the garden which, no longer a "private" *viridarium* or greenery, generally small, as was the custom in the Middle Ages, became, in the Renaissance, the symbol of a prince's power, the scene of parties and plays, a place of relaxation for the court, where one could wander through groves full of allegory, populated with statues, grottoes, fountains. Boboli underwent many alterations owing to variations in taste, but the design remained substantially the same. Near the entrance is the curious Bacchus Fountain in which Valerio Cioli portrayed a dwarf of the court of Cosimo I astride a tortoise; further on is the Grotto by Buontalenti, built between 1583 and 1588 for the eccentric Francesco I; the first chamber is like a real cave in decoration with sculptured forms that, looked at closely, appear as animals; in the corners are four copies of Michelangelo's *Prisoners* (Accademia Gallery) which used to be here; in the cave behind, the group of *Paris and Helena*, by Vincenzo de' Rossi; last comes a small grotto with a *Venus* by Giambologna. Going on one comes to the Amphitheatre, first made in grass in the 16th century and remade in the 18th, for the performance of plays; the obelisk in the centre was brought to Rome from Luxor in the Imperial epoch. Going up to the left one comes to the Neptune fishpond and the Knight's Garden, where the Porcelain Museum is; or going straight on, along a wide avenue, one reaches the beautiful Island Square, with its large pool and island planted with lemon trees and the Ocean Fountain by Giambologna. The garden is full of other antique and Renaissance statues.

At the side: *the entrance to the Ocean Fountain;*
below: *The Ocean Fountain, by Giambologna.*

The church of Santa Maria del Carmine.

SANTA MARIA DEL CARMINE

With Santo Spirito, this is the most important church on the south side of the Arno. It was founded in 1268 by the Carmelite Friars. In 1771 it was burnt down, except for the Corsini and Brancacci chapels and the sacristy; the parts destroyed were completely rebuilt a few years later. The unfinished façade is a high, severe wall of rough stone. The interior is prevalently 18th century; a 17th century masterpiece is the Corsini Chapel, at the end of the left transept, by Silvani and Foggini, with ceiling frescoed by Luca Giordano with the *Apotheosis of St. Andrea Corsini* (1682). At the end of the opposite transept is the main feature of the church: the Brancacci Chapel, whose frescoes mark a crucial moment in the history of Western art. The decoration of the chapel was begun in 1425 for Felice Brancacci, a rich Florentine merchant and diplomat. He commissioned Masolino da Panicale, a painter still sharing the Gothic taste but also open to the new ideas that were beginning to appear in Tuscan painting at the time; and the pioneer, the great master of this renewal was the colleague that Masolino chose to work with him on the Brancacci Chapel, Masaccio. The latter took the older painter's

place perhaps in the following year, when Masolino was called to the court of Hungary, but for reasons unknown, he did not finish the work, which was completed by Filippino Lippi between 1481 and 1485. Masaccio did the best work of his brief career (he died in 1428 at the age of 27) in the Brancacci Chapel: his frescoes won the unconditional admiration of Verrocchio, Fra Angelico, Leonardo, Botticelli, Perugino, Michelangelo and Raphael: his capacity to render the moment pregnant with the event, his historical sense of the Gospel words, his highly expressive dramatic gift, his natural style bare of all superfluous ornament, recall the impact of Giotto, but also make him the first great master of the Italian Renaissance. The cycles of illustrations on the walls of the Brancacci Chapel are two: *Original Sin* and *Scenes from the Life of St. Peter*; among the most significant are the *Expulsion from the Earthly Paradise*, by Masaccio which faces the *Temptation of Adam and Eve*, by Masolino, on the wall opposite; *St Peter heals the lame man and restores Tabitha to life*, by both artists; *St Peter baptises the neophytes*, by Masaccio; *the Payment of the Tribute money*, and *St Peter heals the Sick*, by Masaccio.

Payment of the Tribute, by Masaccio; below, from left to right: *Temptation of Adam and Eve*, by Masolino; *Expulsion from the Earthly Paradise*, by Masaccio.

The church of Santo Spirito on the square of the same name.

SANTO SPIRITO

The church of Santo Spirito stands on the south side of the Arno, in one of the working class districts of the city, and looks on to a simple piazza planted with trees, which is often enlivened by the stalls of a market. The original plan, made by Filippo Brunelleschi in 1444, was for a church facing in the opposite direction, with the façade towards the Arno overlooking a large piazza; but it could not be carried out owing to the opposition of the landowners involved. Brunelleschi's design was largely respected as regards the interior, executed after the master's death by Antonio Manetti and other pupils; while the simple façade is 17th century. The slender, elegant bell-tower was built by Baccio d'Agnolo at the beginning of the 16th century. The spacious and solemn interior recalls the symmetry and rhythmical perfection achieved by Brunelleschi in San Lorenzo, with the variation of a cupola over the presbytery and the continuation of the side aisles in transepts and an apse. The Baroque high altar, an elaborate work by Giovanni Caccini (1608) stands in the centre of the presbytery. In the right transept is a fine *Virgin and Child with Saints and the Commissioners* by Filippo Lippi (c. 1490) with an interesting view of Florence in the background. In the apse is a polyptych by Maso di Banco representing the *Virgin and Child with Saints*; on a nearby altar is a painting of the *Holy Martyrs* by Alessandro Allori (1574); in the predella is a view of the first façade of Pitti Palace. In the left transept is the Corbinelli Chapel, an elegant piece of architecture and sculpture by Andrea Sansovino (1492); next to it is the *Holy Trinity with Sts. Catherine and Magdalen*, attributed to Francesco Granacci. Off the left aisle is an elegant vestibule by Cronaca (1494) with a fine barrel vault; this leads into the beautiful octagonal Sacristy, with cupola, by Giuliano da Sangallo (1492). Leaving the church, on the right is the entrance to the Cenacolo (Last Supper). This was in the refectory of the Augustinian monastery that used to stand here; the wall at the end of the room is covered by a large fresco by Andrea Orcagna (c. 1360) representing two scenes, one above the other: a wonderful *Crucifixion* and a *Last Supper*.

SAN FREDIANO IN CESTELLO

The church was designed by Antonio Ferri, as the elegant cupola (1698); the fine Baroque interior also contains the exquisite *Smiling Madonna*, a coloured wooden statue of the Pisan school, 13th century.

SANTA TRINITA BRIDGE

After Ponte Vecchio, this is certainly the finest and noblest in the city. Built in 1252 and rebuilt several times, it now has the form given it by Bartolomeo Ammannati in 1567-70; at the ends are four statues of the *Seasons*, 1608. The best of these is the one representing *Spring*, by Pietro Francavilla (at the corner with Lungarno Acciaioli).

The church of San Frediano in Cestello; below: *Santa Trinita Bridge.*

The interior of the Santa Trinita Bridge; at the side: *Spini-Ferroni Palace.*

PIAZZA SANTA TRINITA

Surrounded by noble mansions, the piazza is at the beginning of Via Tornabuoni, with the Column of Justice in the centre. This came from the Baths of Caracalla in Rome and supports the statue of Justice by Francesco del Tadda (1581). The fine large battlemented palace that extends as far as Lungarno Acciaioli is the 13th century Palazzo Spini-Ferroni; at No. 1 of the piazza is Palazzo Bartolini-Salimbeni, the masterpiece of Baccio d'Agnolo (1517-20) with cross-shaped windows. The church of Santa Trinita goes back to the 11th century; the Mannerist façade is by Buontalenti (1593-94); the interior is very rich in works of art, that include: a frescoed chapel (fourth on the right) with a painting on wood by Lorenzo Monaco (1420-25), a *Magdalen* in wood by Desiderio da Settignano (1464; fifth chapel on the left); the famous Sassetti Chapel (right transept); the tomb of Benozzo Federighi, a masterpiece by Luca della Robbia (c. 1450, left transept), and in the sacristy, the Renaissance tomb of Onofrio Strozzi, by Piero di Niccolò Lamberti.

The church of Santa Trinita; at the side: *Strozzi Palace.*

STROZZI PALACE

Filippo Strozzi, a Florentine merchant of long-standing wealth (he had the merit of introducing into Tuscany not only the cultivation of artichokes, but also a good variety of fig), commissioned Benedetto da Maiano to build the palace in 1489; Benedetto was succeeded by Cronaca who directed the work until 1504. Later the construction was interrupted and resumed several times; the Strozzi family fell into disfavour in 1538, the palace was confiscated by Cosimo I dei Medici and given back 30 years later. Now it houses the Gabinetto Vieusseux and other cultural organisations; exhibitions are held here periodically, and the biennial Antiques Exhibition Fair. The massive building has a stone plinth all round it at the base, projecting like a bench; the exterior recalls that of Palazzo Medici-Riccardi, with pronounced rustication; at the top is a magnificent cornice by Cronaca; the two upper storeys have fine two-lighted windows; there is a majestic courtyard inside, also by Cronaca.

The church of Ognissanti; at the side: *Saint Jerome in his Study, by Domenico Ghirlandaio.*

OGNISSANTI

The 13th century church of Ognissanti (All Saints) stands in the piazza of the same name overlooking the Arno. It was completely remade in the 17th century. The pleasing Baroque façade is by Matteo Nigetti (1637); the bell-tower is older (14th century). Inside are several paintings on wood and frescoes of the 15th-16th century, including the *Madonna of Mercy*, by Ghirlandaio, commissioned by the Vespucci family (the future great navigator Amerigo also appears in it; 1472). Beside the church is the refectory, with the famous *Last Supper* by Ghirlandaio; there are also two detached frescoes, formerly in the church: *St. Jerome in his study*, also by Ghirlandaio, and *St. Augustine in his study* by Botticelli.

The church of Santa Maria Novella on the square of the same name.

SANTA MARIA NOVELLA

This great Dominican church stands on the site of a 10th century country oratory. It was begun in 1246; the first architects were Fra Sisto and Fra Ristoro. The size of this new church testifies to the importance of the religious orders in Florence at that time, also owing to their vital role as educators: Santa Maria Novella was the seat of the first public school in the city. The façade was begun in 1300, and the lower part was finished before the middle of the century, in the typical Florentine Romanesque - Gothic style. After the middle of the 15th century, Leon Battista Alberti, the great theorist of architecture in the Quattrocento, completed the inlaid marble façade by adding the central doorway and the upper part, of extraordinary elegance, with round window, tympanum and side scrolls. On the right side of the church is a garden, the old Plaona Cemetery, surrounded by sepulchres under Gothic arches. The interior shows the influence of Cistercian Gothic in the "softened" form that this style took in Italy; it is in the form of a Latin cross, with nave and side aisles and composite columns; an incredible number of works of art decorate the

walls and chapels. In the second bay of the right aisle is the tomb of the Blessed Villana, by Bernardo Rossellino (1451); from the last bay one enters the 15th century Pura chapel and from this, the picturesque Cemetery. The right transept leads to the Rucellai Chapel; on the altar is a *Madonna* by Nino Pisano, in the floor the tombstone of Leonardo Dati, by Ghiberti (1425). The chapel of Filippo Strozzi on the right of the high altar is entirely covered with frescoes by Filippo Lippi (c. 1500) with *Stories of Sts. Philip and John*; the tomb of Filippo Strozzi is by Benedetto da Maiano. The chapel of the main altar has frescoes by Domenico Ghirlandaio (c. 1495; the young Michelangelo was probably one of his assistants) with beautiful *Scenes of the Life of the Virgin*. The Gondi Chapel (on the left of the main chapel) has the celebrated *Crucifix* by Brunelleschi, the only sculpture in wood by the master to have remained to us. In the Strozzi Chapel (left transept) are frescoes by Nardo di Cione (c. 1367: remarkable representation of *Hell*). In the Sacristy nearby is a Crucifix, a youthful work by Giotto. Lastly, at the third bay of the left aisle, the marvellous *Trinity* by

Masaccio (c. 1427) and the pulpit designed by Brunelleschi. Going out of the church, on the right, is the interesting group of Cloisters. The 14th century Green Cloister has frescoes in the lunettes by 15th century painters including Paolo Uccello, who executed the *Scenes from Genesis* (very fine is the *Flood*, c. 1430); on one side of the cloister is the entrance to the Spaniards' Chapel, a 14th century chapel frescoed all over, which, in the 16th century, was allocated to the Spaniards at the court of Eleonora di Toledo, the wife of Cosimo I. In the small Cloister of the Dead nearby is a 14th century stained glass window representing the *Coronation of the Virgin*, which used to be in the round window in the façade of the church.

At the side: *the interior of Santa Maria Novella*; below: *Episodes from the life of the Virgin, frescoed by Ghirlandaio in the Sanctuary (details)*; facing page: *frescoes in the Spanish Chapel, by Andrea di Bonaiuto*; above: *Descent into Limbo*; below: *The Church Militant (details)*.

SAN LORENZO

An ancient basilica, consecrated in 393 by St. Ambrose, bishop of Milan, it was probably the first church to be built in the city and was then outside the city walls. Rebuilt in the 11th century, it was radically restored in the 15th century for the Medicis, for whom it was the family church. The interior, spacious, light and elegant, is one of the masterpieces of the early Florentine Renaissance; it is the work of Brunelleschi, who designed it in 1420 and directed the work from 1442 until his death in 1446. It is in the form of a Latin cross and has a nave and two aisles with side chapels. There are numerous masterpieces, including two bronze pulpits by Donatello at the end of the nave, the master's last work (about 1440), completed after his death by pupils; a fine marble tabernacle by Desiderio da Settignano (mid 16th century) opposite the pulpit on the right; the *Marriage of the Virgin*, a painting by Rosso Fiorentino (1523) in the second chapel on the right; a remarkable *Annunciation*, with *Scenes of the life of St. Nicholas of Bari* by Filippo Lippi (c. 1440) in the predella, in the left chapel of the left transept, where, opposite a nineteenth century monument to Donatello (who is buried in the vaults under the church) there is also a curious marble sarcophagus, attributed to Donatello, sculptured like a wicker basket; and also a large fresco representing the *Martyrdom of St. Laurence* by Bronzino (1565-69) in the left aisle, opposite the pulpit. Finally, the Old Sacristy, exceptionally important, for its architecture and works of art, reached from the left transept. Elegant and of crystalline simplicity in its spatial conception, it fully expresses Brunelleschi's architectural idea (1420-29). Despite its small size it ranks as one of Brunelleschi's finest works. It is a chapel on a square plan, composed of a cube surmounted by a hemispherical cupola in sections outlined in pietra serena on white plaster, a decoration typical of Brunelleschi. The eight fine tondi in the lunettes and pendentives (4 with *Scenes from the life of St. John the Evangelist* and 4 with the *Evangelists*) are by Donatello, as are the two bronze doors beside the altar and a fine clay bust of *St. Laurence*; in the centre of the chapel, under a large marble slab, is the *tomb of Giovanni di Bicci dei Medici and of Piccarda Bueri*, the parents of Cosimo the Elder, by Andrea Cavalcanti (1434); on the left wall, under a large arch, is the *Tomb of Piero the Gouty and Giovanni dei Medici*, sons of Cosimo the Elder, by Andrea del Verrocchio.

The exterior and the interior of the Church of San Lorenzo.

LAURENTIAN LIBRARY

This library was founded by Cosimo the Elder and enlarged by Lorenzo the Magnificent; the entrance is in the beautiful cloister of San Lorenzo. It is extraordinarily rich in old manu-scripts and codices. Among the most important are the so-called Medici Virgil (4th-5th century), the Pandects of Justinian (6th century), the oldest existing examples of the tragedies of Aeschylus (11th century) and of the writings of Thucydides, Herodotus and Tacitus (10th century). Michelangelo began the building in 1524 and designed the entrance hall and the large, elegant reading room, while the vestibule was completed by Vasari and other architects.

At the side: *Brunelleschi's Cloister in San Lorenzo;* below: *staircase by Michelangelo in the vestibule of the Laurentian Library.*

The cupola of the Medici Chapels.

MEDICI CHAPELS

The shrine and mausoleum of the Medicis, by the church of San Lorenzo (the entrance is at the back of the church in Piazza Madonna degli Aldobrandini), the Medici chapels are an important architectural and artistic complex, famous above all for the statues by Michelangelo. The Princes' Chapel is also impressive on the outside: its structure resembles that of the Cupola of the Cathedral, octagonal in form with small apses. Inside there is first a wide crypt, which leads to the sumptuous Princes' Chapel, ordered by Ferdinando I in 1602. Work began two years later from a plan by Matteo Nigetti, with the participation of Buontalenti, and continued for more than a century. The great octagon is entirely walled with inlays of hard precious stones and the effect is spectacular. Against the walls are the sarcophagi of six Medici Grand Dukes; above those

of Ferdinando I and Cosimo II, statues in gilt bronze by Ferdinando Tacca; below are sixteen coats of arms of Tuscan cities, also in inlaid hard stones; the cupola is frescoed with *Scenes from the Old and New Testament*, by Pietro Benvenuti (1828). A corridor leads to the *New Sacristy*, the famous and beautiful chapel built by Michelangelo for Cardinal Giulio dei Medici, later Pope Clement VII. It was Michelangelo's first experience in architecture; he worked on it, through various vicissitudes, from 1520 until his patron, who had given him a completely free hand, died and he left Florence for good (1534). However the chapel was not finished. On a square plan, it resembles the structure of Brunelleschi's Old Sacristy, with ribbings in pietra serena on white plaster, but with much richer and more complex architectural decoration (niches, windows,

The interior of the Princes' Chapel; below: *the coats of arms of Florence, Pisa and Siena.*

The interior of the cupola of the Princes' Chapel; below: Madonna and Child, by Michelangelo, flanked by Saint Cosma, by Montorsoli and Saint Damian, by Raffaello da Montelupo.

LORENZO IL MAGNIFICO E GIVLIANO DEI MEDICI

arches etc.). Of the many tombs planned, the only ones completed were those of two minor members of the great Florentine family; Giuliano, Duke of Nemours, the third son of Lorenzo the Magnificent; an expert in political and military affairs, he was appointed by his brother, Pope Leo X, standard bearer of the papal army; he lived for a long time in France, where he received a dukedom from King Francis I, and died at the age of thirty-seven in 1516. The other is Lorenzo, Duke of Urbino, son of Piero the Unfortunate; like his father ill-suited to reign over a state, he received the dukedom of Urbino from his uncle Leo X but reigned for a very short time. He made a political marriage to a relation of the King of France, Madeleine de la Tour d'Auvergne, (1518). The two twin tombs are seen against the splendid architecture: sculptured figures of the two men are placed over the sarcophagi, which are decorated with the famous allegorical statues. On the left, with his back to the altar, is *Giuliano* represented as an antique warrior in a cuirass, sublimely idealised; there is a story that when people told Michelangelo that the statue did not look at all like the deceased, as appears evident from the paintings by Allori and Bronzino, he said that after ten centuries no-one would notice. On the sarcophagus are the figures of *Night*, reclining in sleep, and *Day*, muscular, vigorous, with strangely twisted limbs, the face unfinished. *Lorenzo*, on the right, is in a noble meditative posture (he is called "Il Pensieroso") with a warlike helmet on his head; at his feet, the melancholy dozing *Dusk* and the awakening *Dawn*, perhaps the most famous, the finest of all these statues. Over the sarcophagus containing the remains of Lorenzo the Magnificent and his brother Giuliano, killed in the Pazzi conspiracy, is the beautiful *Virgin and Child*, also by Michelangelo, at which the two dukes gaze; at the sides, *St. Cosma* (left) by Montorsoli and *St. Damian* (right) by Raffaello da Montelupo, works by two pupils of Michelangelo that fall far below the expressive achievement of the statues near them. This work by Michelangelo, though unfinished (the tomb of Lorenzo the Magnificent and Giuliano was finished off by Vasari) is generally interpreted as a lofty meditation on human destiny, its vanity and its redemption by religious faith. The three zones of the chapel can be understood in this sense: the lower order, with the tombs and allegorical statues, represents all-consuming Time that leads inexorably to death, to Hades; the middle band is the terrestrial sphere, and the upper one, more luminous, with the lunettes and the cupola, the vault of Heaven: the sarcophagi are as it were interrupted in the middle by scrolls, thus liberating the souls of the deceased which go beyond every dimension in space and time, to their redemption by the eternal idea of Life (the Virgin and Child).

Two works by Michelangelo: left: *the Tomb of Giuliano, duke of Nemours;* right: *the Tomb of Lorenzo, duke of Urbino.*

The statues of Night (above) and Day (below), on the Tomb of Giuliano, by Michelangelo.

The statues of Dusk (above) *and Dawn* (below), *on the Tomb of Lorenzo, by Michelangelo.*

PALAZZO MEDICI - RICCARDI

Built for Cosimo the Elder in Via Larga, now Via Cavour, between 1444 and 1460, by the Florentine architect and sculptor Michelozzo Michelozzi, this was the prototype of all Florentine palaces of the Renaissance. Majestic and elegant, it was filled with works of art commissioned by the Medicis; the main branch of the family lived there until 1540. In 1655 the palace was sold to the Riccardi family and is now the seat of the provincial administration and the Prefettura. Exhibitions and other cultural events often take place here. It was designed by Michelozzo as a large cube, and must have stood out among the lower buildings round it; but the Riccardi family had it enlarged, adding seven new windows on Via Larga. The two principal sides, carefully designed by the architect with a view to the pictorial effect of the volumes, have pronounced rustication on the ground floor, flatter rustication on the storey above and smooth stones on the third. This motif was to reappear frequently for more than a century, along with the use of two-lighted windows with round arches. There is a fine classical cornice, while the big corner windows (called "kneeling windows" from the form of the corbels) which took the place of a

At the side: the facade of Palazzo Medici-Riccardi; below: Michelozzo's courtyard in the palace.

104

The Journey of the Three Kings to Bethlehem, by Benozzo Gozzoli (detail); at the side: *view of the Chapel of Palazzo Medici-Riccardi.*

previously existing loggia, are attributed to Michelangelo (c. 1517). On the same corner is a large Medici coat of arms, which, according to Benvenuto Cellini, was originally brightly coloured; seven red balls on a gold ground. Inside the palace is a fine courtyard, with porticoes, that contains Roman remains and various pieces of sculpture. The second courtyard, which was also very magnificent and where receptions and shows were held on the occasion of weddings and celebrations, has been rebuilt unsuccessfully. This palace used to contain many of the masterpieces that are now on view in the galleries and museums of Florence. Among the various rooms, important is the Chapel by Michelozzo, reached by going up the first staircase on the right in the courtyard. Here are the celebrated frescoes by Benozzo Gozzoli representing the *Journey of the Three Kings to Bethlehem* (1459-60) in which many personages of the time are portrayed: Lorenzo the Magnificent with his father, Piero the Gouty and his sisters, Galeazzo Maria Sforza, Sigismondo Malatesta, John VII Paleologus, Emperor of Constantinople, the painter himself and his master, Fra Angelico. There is also a Gallery, reached by going up the second stairs, decorated with stuccoes and mirrors of the end of the 18th century, with a fresco by Luca Giordano on the vault, the *Apotheosis of the Medici dynasty* (1682-83).

The church of San Marco.

SAN MARCO

Piazza San Marco has a prevalently modern look; the only medieval note is the 14th century loggia of the Accademia, once part of the former Hospital of St. Matthew, and now the entrance portico of the Academy of Fine Arts. On the corner with Via degli Arazzieri is the Palace of Livia (1775), built by Grand Duke Pietro Leopoldo for a circus dancer, Livia Malfatti. In the centre of the piazza are shrubs and trees and a monument to General Manfredo Fanti, by Pio Fedi (1873). One side of the piazza is occupied by the church and monastery of San Marco. There was a monastery of Silvestrini monks here from 1299 onwards; in the first half of the 15th century Cosimo the Elder assigned both the church and the monastery to the reformed Dominican monks of the Blessed Giovanni Dominici; this was partly by the desire of Pope Eugene IV, and partly in expiation of Cosimo's own misdeeds. He commissioned Michelozzo to carry out the work of restoration. In the following centuries there were several alterations, particularly to the church, which has now a late 18th century façade in a neo-cinquecento style. The interior was re-structured by Giambologna in 1588 and by Silvani in 1678; on the interior façade is a *Crucifix* by followers of Giotto; at the third altar on the right, a *Virgin in prayer* (Mosaic).

The interior of the church of San Marco; below: the Cloister of Saint Antoninus, by Michelozzo.

Enthroned Madonna and Child with Saints, by Fra Angelico.

MUSEUM OF SAN MARCO

The entrance to the monastery of San Marco is beside the church. This was one of the most important centres in Florence in the 15th century, thanks to the favour it held with Cosimo the Elder and Lorenzo the Magnificent, the unquestioned authority of its prior, St. Antonino, and the fact that it housed Savonarola, Fra Angelico and Fra Bartolomeo. Fra Angelico was one of the greatest artists of the 15th century; he infused the new, robust form inherited from Masaccio with a spirit that was still Gothic. The Cloister of St. Antonino, by Michelozzo, has frescoed lunettes and there are some rooms opening on to it; The Pilgrims' Hospice contains a series of paintings on wood by Fra Angelico: the *Flax-growers' tabernacle*, the *altar-piece from the convent of Bosco ai Frati*, the *Annalena altar-piece*, the *Descent from the Cross*, the *Last Judgement*. The Chapter-house contains a *Crucifixion* by Fra Angelico. The artist also decorated the Dormitory; the series of cells has such masterpieces as the *Annunciation*, *Noli me tangere*, the *Transfiguration* and the *Coronation of the Virgin*. In the Prior's Apartment is a *Portrait of Savonarola*, who lived in these rooms, by Fra Bartolomeo.

Saint Domenic at the Foot of the Crucifix, by Fra Angelico.

Above: *Annunciation, by Fra Angelico;* at the side: *Flight into Egypt, panel of the door of the Silver Cupboard, by Fra Angelico.* Facing page, above from the left: *Noli me tangere, by Fra Angelico;* Crucifixion with the Virgin, Saint Domenic and Angels, by a collaborator of Fra Angelico; below: *Virgin and Child Enthroned with Saints, by Fra Angelico.*

The church of the Santissima Annunziata and the Monument to Grand-duke Ferdinand I; below: small marble temple, by Michelozzo, which houses the Annunciation, of Florentine school.

SANTISSIMA ANNUNZIATA

In 1250 seven young Florentines, later beatified as the Seven Saints, founded the order of the Servites, or Servants of Mary, and began to build a shrine dedicated to the Virgin. The church was rebuilt by Michelozzo in the 15th century, and later by Antonio Manetti who, with the collaboration of Leon Battista Alberti, concluded the design of the circular Tribune at the end of the single nave. The porch on the piazza is late 16th century. Between this and the church is the Cloister of Vows, decorated with fine early 16th century frescoes by Andrea del Sarto, Pontormo, Rosselli, Franciabigio and other Mannerists. Inside the church, which was restored and embellished in the Baroque period, is a small 15th century Temple, immediately on the left on entering, that contains a greatly venerated 14th century Florentine school *Annunciation*, which legend attributed to the hand of an angel. Among the many works of art, mention should be made of two lecterns in the form of eagles (15th century English work) in the elegant Tribune; *Jesus and St. Julian* by Andrea del Castagno (c. 1455, first altar on the left) and the *Trinity* by the same.

The Hospital of the Holy Innocents; below: *the Cloister of the Hospital of the Holy Innocents.*

HOSPITAL OF THE HOLY INNOCENTS

In 1419 the Guild of Silk Merchants decided to purchase a piece of land and build a hospital to receive the foundlings or "Innocents", that is, children who had been abandoned. Brunelleschi was commissioned to provide the plan, by which he determined the architecture of the whole piazza on which the hospital faces, creating a portico whose proportions in relation to the rest required the uniformity of all the buildings erected there. The hospital was finished in 1457; the front consists of nine wide arches on columns that stand at the top of a flight of steps; above these, a low upper storey which has windows with a tympanum; between the arches, glazed terracotta tondi by Andrea della Robbia (c. 1487); two pilaster strips close the portico at the side. Inside are the cloisters by Brunelleschi and a gallery of works mostly of the 15th century. The collection includes: an *Annunciation* by Giovanni del Biondo; *Adoration of the Magi* by Ghirlandaio (1488); a *Madonna and Child with Angels* by the school of Perugino.

ARCHAEOLOGICAL MUSEUM

Cosimo the Elder was a keen collector of coins, goldsmiths' work and antique sculptures, a passion shared by the later Medicis. The Lorraine family began the collection of Egyptian antiquities, and encouraged independent excavation; in 1828 Leopoldo II subsidized an archaeological expedition in Egypt and Nubia. In 1880 the collection was housed in its present seat, Palazzo della Crocetta in Via della Colonna. The museum is divided into three sections: the Etrurian Topographical Museum, the Etrusco-Graeco-Roman Antiquities, and the Egyptian Collection. On the ground floor are two rooms arranged didactically: the *François vase* and the *Mater Matuta* are kept here. The garden contains reconstructions, partly with authentic materials, of funeral monuments and Etruscan tombs. The Egyptian Collection is on the first floor. Among the most interesting exhibits: the two statuettes of handmaidens intent on domestic work; the statue of *Thutmosi* III (1490-1436 B.C.); the "Fayyum" portrait of a woman (2nd century A.D.). On the first floor; Attic *kouroi* of the 6th century B.C.; the statue of the *Orator* (c. 100 B.C.); the *Chimaera of Arezzo*; the *Small Idol*.

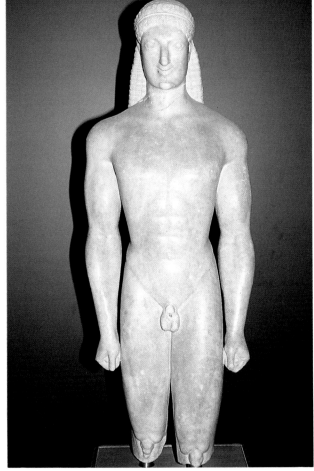

At the side: *wooden statuette, Egyptian art (ca 2400 B.C.)*; below: *Chimaera, Etruscan art (4th century B.C.)*. Preceding page, above: *the François Vase, a magnificent example of Attic Black-figure pottery, signed by the potter Ergotimos and the painter Kleitias*; below, from left to right: *the Mater Matuta, an Etruscan sculpture (second half of the 5th cent. B.C.); Attic kouros (6th cent. B.C.)*.

The "Tribune", by Emilio de' Fabris; facing page: David, by Michelangelo.

GALLERY OF THE ACCADEMIA

This is one of the most famous galleries in Italy, visited by thousands of people, especially owing to the presence of the *David* and of other famous sculptures by Michelangelo. The Gallery, (Via Ricasoli 60, near Piazza San Marco) was founded in 1784 by Grand Duke Pietro Leopoldo of Lorraine; at the same time the Academy of Fine Arts was instituted, to unite all the schools of art, drawing and sculpture already existing in the city; so the gallery was created with the specific purpose of helping the pupils to know and to study the Old Masters. Many of the works, however, came from a previous collection, that belonged to the Academy of the Art of Drawing, an institution of great prestige, founded in 1562 by Cosimo I. This included all the greatest artists of the time, and was based on the example of the 14th century Company of Painters of St. Luke. The collection of paintings, already consid-

erable, was increased as a result of the suppression of churches and monasteries (1786 and 1808); there were further acquisitions and in 1873 the *David* was brought here, followed in 1911 by the *Prisoners* and *St. Matthew*, while the *Pietà* only arrived in 1939, after its recovery from the antiques market. The Gallery also exhibits plaster models by Giambologna. There is a notable collection of paintings from the 13th till the early 16th century; among the most important works are: a *Crucifix*, Sienese school, second half of the 13th century (attributed by some people to the great Duccio di Buoninsegna); the *Tree of the Cross*, by Pacino di Buonaguida (early 14th century); a polyptych by Andrea Orcagna (mid 14th century) and works by his brothers, including a triptych by Nardo di Cione (1365) and a *Coronation of the Virgin* by Jacopo di Cione; 24 panels by Taddeo Gaddi (14 with *Scenes of the Life of Christ*

Gallery of the Accademia, room with the Rape of the Sabine Women, by Giambologna; at the side: *Madonna and Child, the Infant Saint John and Two Angels, by Sandro Botticelli.* Preceding page: the *Four Prisoners, by Michelangelo;* above, left to right: *the Prisoner known as Atlas, the Young Prisoner, the Prisoner Awakening and the Bearded Prisoner* (the first at the bottom left); below, centre: *Saint Matthew, by Michelangelo;* below, right: *Palestrina Pietà, by Michelangelo.*

and 10 with *Scenes of the life of St. Francis;* the very fine *Pietà* by Giovanni da Milano (1365); the *Adimari Chest;* a *Visitation* attributed to Domenico Ghirlandaio; the *Madonna of the Sea* and the youthful *Madonna and Child, little St. John and two Angels,* by Sandro Botticelli; *Trinity and Saints,* by Alessio Baldovinetti (1471).

Monument to Michelangelo at the centre of Piazzale Michelangelo.

PIAZZALE MICHELANGELO

On the south side of the Arno, going along Viale Michelangelo or else walking up the ramps that go up from the San Niccolò gate, one comes to a large panoramic terrace, which affords a view over the whole town and the surrounding hills: Piazzale Michelangelo. This large area was conceived by Giuseppe Poggi in the 1860's as the scenographic climax to his work of "redesigning" the town;

Florence was then the capital of Italy. In the centre of the square is the monument to Michelangelo erected in 1875 with copies in bronze of some of his marble statues. Going on up the hill, behind Piazzale Michelangelo, is the beautiful little church of San Salvatore al Monte, begun by Cronaca in 1495. Inside there appears for the first time in the Renaissance a double order of columns, superimposed.

Two views of Piazzale Michelangelo.

San Miniato al Monte; facing page: *the interior.*

SAN MINIATO AL MONTE

One of the oldest and most beautiful churches in Florence, it stands on the site of the first Christian settlements in the city, the old *Mons Florentinus*, where the woods were full, first of catacombs, then of oratories and the little hovels of monks. One oratory was dedicated to San Miniato, who suffered martyrdom on the hill in the 4th century, and the Romanesque church was built over this in the 11th-13th century. The façade is covered with marble in two colours, in a clear, solemn design; the fine mosaic in the centre (13th century, much restored) represents *Christ between the Virgin and St. Miniato;* at the top of the tympanum, *the Eagle,* the symbol of the Guild of Woolmerchants whose task it was to organize the upkeep of the church. The interior has a nave and two side aisles, with a crypt and a raised presbytery above it; the floor of the

nave is set with splendid slabs of inlaid marble. In the centre, between the two flights of steps leading up to the presbytery, is the Crucifix Chapel, by Michelozzo (1448), commissioned by Piero the Gouty, the father of Lorenzo the Magnificent. The chapel was built to house a famous Crucifix which miraculously nodded to St. Giovanni Gualberto and is now in Santa Trinita; the vault has coffers by Luca della Robbia; on the end wall, panels painted by Angolo Gaddi. From the left aisle one enters the Chapel of the Cardinal of Portugal, one of the most elegant creations of the Florentine Renaissance, by Antonio Manetti (1461-66) a pupil of Brunelleschi; this contains the tomb of Jacopo Di Lusitania, archbishop of Lisbon, by Rossellino; fine della Robbia terracottas on the vault, a splendid *Annunciation* by Baldovinetti (on the left) and two *angels*

Christ Enthroned between the Virgin and Saint Minias with the Symbols of the Evangelists.

frescoed by Antonio and Piero del Pollaiolo (on the wall at the end, above the copy of the *Saints Eustace, James and Vincent* by Antonio and Piero, which is now at the Uffizi). On the vault of the crypt, above the altar, are frescoes of *Saints and Prophets* by Taddeo Gaddi. The presbytery of the church is surrounded with fine 13th century marble parapets on which is the elegant pulpit; on the right altar is a painting on wood by Jacopo del Casentino with *St. Miniato and eight scenes of his life*; the mosaic in the apse represents *Christ enthroned between the Virgin, St. Miniato and the symbols of the Evangelists* (1279, but restored in 1491 by Baldovinetti). From the Presbytery one goes on the right to the Sacristy, frescoed after 1387 by Spinello Aretino, with *Stories of St. Benedict*; the door next to that of the Sacristy leads into the Cloister, with the remains of frescoes by Andrea del Castagno and, in the loggia above, by Paolo Uccello. On the right of the church is the Bishops' Palace (13th-14th century). Round the church are the walls of the Fortress erected by Michelangelo in 1529.

Fort Belvedere; at the side: *Porta San Giorgio.*

FORT BELVEDERE

Perched on the top of the hill of St. George, the fort is the highest point in Florence, and the splendid views one enjoys from its parapets in all directions fully justify the Fort's name of Belvedere (beautiful view). Already envisaged as a fort in the Duke of Athens' time, before his expulsion from Florence, it was finally commenced in 1590, by order of Ferdinand Ist de' Medici, to designs by the famous military engineer, Bernardo Buontalenti. The Fort was designed to defend the city from the South and to protect the grand-ducal family in times of civil unrest. The governor of the Fort's residence is, at present, used for internationally renowned exhibitions.

FIESOLE

A charming little town about 4 miles north of Florence, it was founded by the Etruscans in the 4th century B.C.; three centuries later it was conquered by the Romans. After the fall of the Empire it was an important bishopric; in the 12th century it succumbed to its stronger neighbour, Florence. Having lost all its political power, it came to be, with time, a favourite summer resort for rich Florentines (also the Medicis had a villa there) and, in the 19th century, also for foreign visitors, especially the English. The centre of the little town is Piazza Mino, where the principal public buildings are. The Cathedral was erected in 1028 and later enlarged in 1256 and 1300; in the Salutati Chapel are frescoes by Cosimo Rosselli and the tomb of Bishop Leonardo Salutati, by Mino da Fiesole, 15th century; on the High Altar is a triptych by Bicci di Lorenzo (c. 1440); in the crypt, which is Romanesque, are 15th century frescoes by Benedetto di Nanni, a baptismal font by Francesco del Tadda (16th century) and the wooden Bishop's Chair by Andrea Corsini (14th century). The Bandini Museum nearby has interesting Della Robbia terracottas and works by Agnolo and Taddeo Gaddi, Lorenzo Monaco and Jacopo del Sellaio. Also in Piazza Mino is the Praetorian Palace (15th century) with façade and loggia covered with coats of arms. Near the piazza is the Roman theatre (1st century B.C.) which seats an audience of 3000 and is still in use for summer concerts and other performances. In the vicinity of the theatre are the remains of a temple (first Etruscan and later Roman) and some Roman baths. The Archaeological Museum beside the area of excavation contains relics of Etruscan and Roman Fiesole; urns from Chiusi and Volterra; storied stelae, typical of the zone; Greek vases, objects in *bucchero*, small bronzes. Returning to the piazza, one goes up a very steep little road to Sant'Alessandro, an ancient church standing on the site of an Etruscan temple. A little beyond it are the church and monastery of San Francesco; this church was built between the 14th and 15th century, and has a simple façade with a rose-window and suspended porch. The interior is Gothic with a single nave; the High Altar has a beautiful *Annunciation* by Raffaellino del Garbo (early 16th century); at the second altar on the left, *Madonna and Saints* by the school of Perugino; next to it, a *Conception* by Cosimo Rosselli; a fine early 16th century inlaid choir. On the right of the church is the small Cloister of St. Bernardino (13th-14th century). Half way between Fiesole and Florence is the church of San Domenico, built in the 15th century; it contains a *Madonna and Child with Angels and Saints* by Fra Angelico (c. 1430).

Piazza Mino da Fiesole.

The church of San Francesco; below: *the Roman theatre.*